MONDAY

TUESDAY

WEDNESDAY

THURSDAY

FRIDAY

SATURDAY

SUNDAY

The Calendar

How Long Is a WEEK?

by Claire Clark

Consulting editor: Gail Saunders-Smith, PhD

CAPSTONE PRESS
a capstone imprint

Pebble Plus is published by Capstone Press,
1710 Roe Crest Drive, North Mankato, Minnesota 56003.
www.capstonepub.com

Books published by Capstone Press are manufactured with paper
containing at least 10 percent post-consumer waste.

Library of Congress Cataloging-in-Publication Data
Clark, Claire, 1973–
  How long is a week? / by Claire Clark.
    p. cm. — (Pebble Plus. The calendar)
  Summary: "Uses simple text and photos to explain a week as a unit of time and the days of the week"—Provided by
publisher.
  Includes bibliographical references and index.
  ISBN 978-1-4296-7592-5 (library binding)
  ISBN 978-1-4296-7900-8 (paberback)
  1. Week—Juvenile literature. I. Title.
  CE13.C55 2012
  529—dc23   2011021345

Editorial Credits
Kristen Mohn, editor; Bobbie Nuytten, designer; Marcie Spence, media researcher; Marcy Morin, studio scheduler;
    Kathy McColley, production specialist

Photo Credits
Capstone Studio: Karon Dubke

Note to Parents and Teachers

The Calendar series supports national science and social studies standards related to time.
This book describes and illustrates what makes a week. The images support early readers in
understanding the text. The repetition of words and phrases helps early readers learn new
words. This book also introduces early readers to subject-specific vocabulary words, which are
defined in the Glossary section. Early readers may need assistance to read some words and to
use the Table of Contents, Glossary, Read More, Internet Sites, and Index sections of the book.

Printed in the United States of America in North Mankato, Minnesota.
102011   006405CGS12

Table of Contents

What Is a Week?

It's National Pizza Week!

How long does it last?

A week is seven days in a row.

Seven days of pizza!

Monday	Tuesday	Wednesday	Thursday	Friday	Saturday
	1	2	3	4	5
8	9	10	11	12	
14	15	16	17	18	19
21	22	23	24	25	26
28	29	30			

pizza week!

Long ago, people in Rome
and China decided seven days
would be a week. There are
52 weeks in one year.

Rome

China

Days of the Week

On a calendar, a week begins on Sunday. It ends on Saturday. The five days in between are often called school days or weekdays.

MONDAY
TUESDAY
WEDNESDAY
THURSDAY
FRIDAY

The weekend is made up
of Saturday and Sunday.
What do you like to do
on the weekend?

A week can start on any day. You might visit your grandpa for one week. If you arrive on Wednesday, you could stay until Tuesday.

What Lasts a Week?

Some vacations last a week.

Spring break is often one week.

Weather can last a week.
Sometimes rain falls all
week long.

Showers

Partly Sunny
with Showers

Wednesday	Thursday	Friday	Saturday	Sunday

| Showers | Thunderstorms | Partly Sunny with Showers | Partly Cloudy with Chance of Showers | Thunderstorms |

Illness can last a week.
You might have a cold
for a week. Next week
you'll feel better!

Pizza Week is the
second week of January.
It is the best seven days
of the year!

Glossary

calendar—a chart that shows all of the days, weeks, and months in a year

illness—sickness

spring break—time off from school in spring

vacation—a trip away from home

weekday—a day of the week except Saturday and Sunday; a weekday is often a school day or a work day

weekend—Saturday and Sunday, or the two days at the end of the school week or work week

Read More

Adamson, Thomas K., and Heather Adamson. *How Do You Measure Time?* Measure It! Mankato, Minn.: Capstone Press, 2011.

Levine, Arthur A. *Monday Is One Day*. New York: Scholastic Press, 2011.

Steffora, Tracey. *Days of the Week*. Measuring Time. Chicago: Heinemann Library, 2011.

Internet Sites

FactHound offers a safe, fun way to find Internet sites related to this book. All of the sites on FactHound have been researched by our staff.

Here's all you do:

Visit *www.facthound.com*

Type in this code: 9781429675925

 Check out projects, games and lots more at **www.capstonekids.com**

Index

Word Count: 166
Grade: 1
Early-Intervention Level: 19